ROUND AND ROUND THE SEASONS

This book is dedicated to all children
who love nature and enjoy poetry

Round and Round the Seasons

Poems to Enjoy All the Year Through

COMPILED BY PAT WYNNEJONES

ILLUSTRATED BY GILL SAMPSON

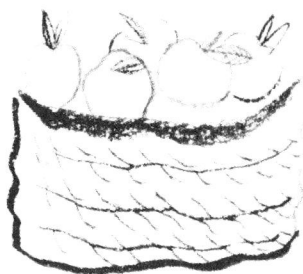

A LION BOOK

Published by
Lion Publishing plc
Sandy Lane West, Oxford, England
ISBN 0 7459 3381 5

First edition 1997
10 9 8 7 6 5 4 3 2 1 0

A catalogue record for this book is available
from the British Library

Printed and bound in Spain by Bookprint

Contents

INTRODUCTION

'In winter I get up at night
And dress by yellow candle-light.
In summer quite the other way,
I have to go to bed by day.'

The seasons affect the clothes we wear, the things we do and
the world we live in. Wouldn't life be dull if winter and summer
were just the same? I have chosen these poems because they
help us to see more clearly the beauty and variety of the changing
seasons and to reflect on how we celebrate some special times
of the year. As a Christian, I believe that God is the maker of 'all
things great and small'; many of these poems reveal something
about the one who made our world and who set the seasons in
motion.

In the Bible, King Solomon said that the seeing eye and the
hearing ear are 'gifts' from God. Poems can make these gifts
special by showing us things from another angle. They can bring
fresh ways of seeing and give birth to new thoughts and ideas.
They open up a wider field of vision.

Have you ever wanted to say something, but been unable to
find the words? Perhaps these poems will help you. Some were
written by people who lived a long time ago, others by modern
poets, and a few by today's children—they all share the same
love of nature and of the sound of words. Some capture the
feeling of the changing seasons, and some celebrate times of
special joy during the Christian year. There is something here
for everyone, and I hope that these poems will be a lasting
source of pleasure. This book is one that you can enjoy with a
friend, but I especially hope that, when you read it alone, the
poems themselves will become your friends.

PAT WYNNEJONES

Seasons

SEASONS

Spring, summer, autumn, winter,
Every year the same—
Round and round the seasons go
Like a party game.
Spin the leaves from green to brown
Spin them on to gold,
Turn the weather up to hot
Turn it down to cold.
Chase the clouds across the sky
Paint a yellow sun,
Then the rail comes tumbling down
Spoiling all our fun.

Spring, summer, autumn, winter,
Every year the same—
Round and round the seasons go
Like a party game.

Steve Turner

SEASONS

In Springtime when the leaves are young,
Clear dewdrops gleam like jewels, hung,
On boughs the fair birds roost among.

When Summer comes with sweet unrest,
Birds weary of their mother's breast
And look abroad and leave the nest.

In Autumn ere the waters freeze,
The swallows fly across the seas:—
If we could fly away with these!

In Winter when the birds are gone,
The sun himself looks starved and wan,
And starved the snow he shines upon.

Christina Rossetti

ALL SEASONS SHALL BE SWEET

Therefore all seasons shall be sweet to thee,
Whether the summer clothe the general earth
With greenness, or redbreast sit and sing
Betwixt the tufts of snow on the bare branch
Of mossy apple-tree, while the nigh thatch
Smokes in the sun-thaw; whether the eave-drops fall
Heard only in the trances of the blast,
Or if the secret ministry of frost
Shall hang them up in silent icicles,
Quietly shining to the quiet moon.

S.T. Coleridge

THAW

Over the land freckled with snow half-thawed
The speculating rooks at their nests cawed
And saw from the elm-tops, delicate as flower of grass,
What we below could not see, Winter pass.

Edward Thomas

SPRING

Look, the winter is past.
The rains are over and gone.
Blossoms appear through all the land.
The time has come to sing.
The cooing of doves is heard in our land.

King Solomon

A Change in the Year

It is the first mild day of March:
Each minute sweeter than before,
The redbreast sings from the tall larch
That stands beside our door.

There is a blessing in the air,
Which seems a sense of joy to yield
To the bare trees, and mountains bare,
And grass in the green field.

William Wordsworth

The Kiss of Spring

Who but You O God can rescue the earth
from the grip of winter?
You take the bare fields, bleak and desolate
and dress them in green,
splashing us with colours,
reminding us that Life comes
through You.
All about me buds are bursting,
I am dwarfed by Your great universe
when spring arrives.

Tammy Felton

April Rise

If ever I saw blessing in the air
I see it now in this still early day
Where lemon-green the vaporous morning drips
Wet sunlight on the powder of my eye.

Blown bubble-film of blue, the sky wraps round
Weeds of warm light whose every root and rod
Splutters with soapy green, and all the world
Sweats with the bead of summer in its bud.

If ever I heard blessing it is there
Where birds in trees that shoals and shadows are
Splash with their hidden wings and drops of sound
Break on my ears their crests of throbbing air.

Pure in the haze the emerald sun dilates,
The lips of sparrows milk the mossy stones,
While white as water by the lake a girl
Swims her green hand among the gathered swans.

Now, as the almond burns its smoking wick,
Dropping small flames to light the candled grass:
Now, as my low blood scales its second chance,
If ever world were blessed, now it is.

Laurie Lee

LITTLE BROWN SEED

Little brown seed, round and sound,
Here I put you in the ground.

You can sleep a week or two,
Then—I'll tell you what to do:

You must grow some downward roots,
Then some tiny upward shoots.

From those green shoots folded sheaves
Soon must come some healthy leaves.

When the leaves have time to grow,
Next a bunch of buds must show.

Last of all the buds must spread
Into blossoms white or red.

There, seed! I've done my best—
Please to grow and do the rest.

Rodney Bennett

Spring Prayer

For flowers that bloom about our feet;
For tender grass, so fresh, so sweet;
For song of bird and hum of bee;
For all things fair we hear or see,
Father in heaven, we thank Thee!

For blue of stream and blue of sky;
For pleasant shade of branches high;
For fragrant air and cooling breeze;
For beauty of the blooming trees,
Father in heaven, we thank Thee.

Ralph W. Emerson

GREEN AND GROWING THINGS

We'll go to the meadows where cowslips do grow,
And buttercups, looking as yellow as gold;
And daisies and violets beginning to blow;
For it is a most beautiful sight to behold.

The little bee humming about them is seen,
The butterfly merrily dances along;
The grasshopper chirps in the hedges so green,
And the linnet is singing his liveliest song.

The birds and the insects are happy and gay,
The beasts of the field they are glad and rejoice,
And we will be thankful to God every day,
And praise his great name in a loftier voice.

He made the green meadows, he planted the flowers.
He sent his great sun in the heavens to blaze;
He created these wonderful bodies of ours,
And as long as we live we will sing of his praise.

Jane or Ann Taylor

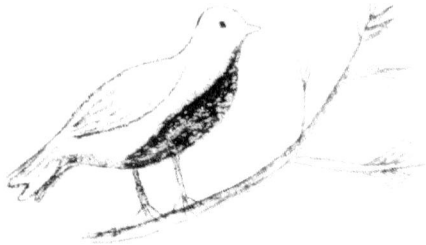

SPRING HAS COME

Now the spring has come again, joy and warmth will follow;
Cold and wet are quite forgot, northward flies the swallow;
Over sea and land and air spring's soft touch is everywhere
And the world looks cleaner;
All our sinews feel new strung, hearts are light that once
    were wrung,
Youthful zests are keener.

All the woods are new in leaf, all the fruit is budding,
Bees are humming round the hive, done with
    winter's brooding;
Seas are calm and blue again, clouds no more foretell
    the rain
Winds are soft and tender;
High above, the kingly sun laughs once more his course
    to run,
Shines in all his splendour.

God is in the midst of her, God commands her duty;
Earth does but reflect his light, mirrors back his beauty;
God's the fount whence all things flow, great and small,
    above, below,
God's their only maker:
We but poorer patterns are of that mind beyond compare,
    God our great creator.

Tr. Steuart Wilson
'IN VERNALI TEMPORE' PIAE CANTIONES 1582

God's Plan for Spring

It never has failed, and it never will,
The wind swings around and the violets come;
There's a touch of green on a bare gray hill,
And the robin is building himself a home.

Year after year, year after year—
That is the way that God has planned—
We feel a loveliness somewhere near,
And spring comes moving across the land.

Boughs grow heavy with leaf and bud,
The sky is a sea with drifting sails;
And spring comes back, as we knew she would,
That is God's plan and it never fails.

Nancy Byrd Turner

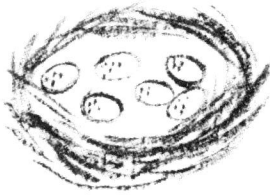

SPRING

Nothing is so beautiful as spring—
When weeds, in wheels, shoot long and lovely and lush;
Thrush's eggs look little low heavens, and thrush
Through the echoing timber does so rinse and wring
The ear, it strikes like lightnings to hear him sing;
The glassy pear-tree leaves and blooms, they brush
The descending blue; that blue is all in a rush
With richness; the racing lambs too have fair their fling.

What is all this juice and all this joy?
A strain of the earth's sweet being in the beginning
In Eden garden. —Have, get, before it cloy,
Before it cloud, Christ, lord, and sour with sinning,
Innocent mind and Mayday in girl and boy,
Most, O Maid's child, thy choice and worthy the winning.

Gerard Manley Hopkins

DAFFODILS

I wandered lonely as a cloud
That floats on high o'er vales and hills,
When all at once I saw a crowd,
A host, of golden daffodils;
Beside the lake, beneath the trees,
Fluttering and dancing in the breeze.

Continuous as the stars that shine
And twinkle on the milky way,
They stretched in never-ending line
Along the margin of a bay:
Ten thousand saw I at a glance,
Tossing their heads in sprightly dance.

The waves beside them danced; but they
Out-did the sparkling waves in glee:
A poet could not but be gay,
In such a jocund company:
I gazed—and gazed—but little thought
What wealth the show to me had brought:

For oft, when on my couch I lie
In vacant or in pensive mood,
They flash upon that inward eye
Which is the bliss of solitude;
And then my heart with pleasure fills,
And dances with the daffodils.

William Wordsworth

Summer Memories

The rays of an invigorating summer's day
filter into my room,
The sweet smells of harvesting
drift through my slightly open window,
The superabundant range of colours
in the flowers and trees.

The rhythmic beating of
a passing train,
The friendly, inviting hum of
bees about their busy work,
The novel chirping of birds as they
sing their summer's greeting.

The soft, sweet breezes
making curtains flitter
The sparkling crystal clear waterfalls
winding in and out of forgotten rocks,
The fluttering butterfly with its
elegant beautiful silk wings.

All these are my memories of summer.

Robert Fanshawe (aged 16)

BED IN SUMMER

In winter I get up at night
And dress by yellow candle-light.
In summer quite the other way,
I have to go to bed by day.

I have to go to bed and see
The birds still hopping on the tree,
Or hear the grown-up people's feet
Still going past me in the street.

And does it not seem hard to you,
When all the sky is clear and blue,
And I should like so much to play,
To have to go to bed by day?

Robert Louis Stevenson

SUMMER SEA

Walking out from the cool verdant forest
Into the heat of the bright summer's day,
Sinking my toes in the soft white sand whilst
Gazing out across the endless sapphire sea,
I licked the salt from my lips
As I listened to the gentle lazy murmur of the waves,
Rolling against the nose of rocks
Pushing out into the sea

Iain M. Barker (aged 16)

AT THE SEA-SIDE

When I was down beside the sea,
A wooden spade they gave to me
To dig the sandy shore.

My holes were empty like a cup,
In every hole the sea came up,
Till it could come no more.

Robert Louis Stevenson

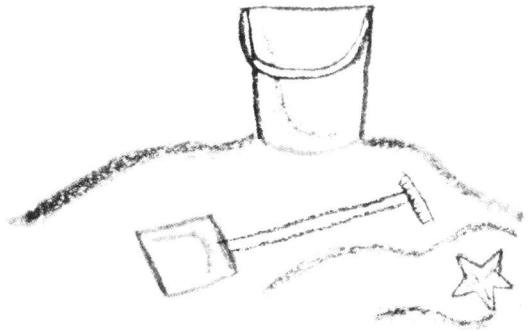

SAND-BETWEEN-THE-TOES

I went down to the shouting sea,
Taking Christopher down with me,
For Nurse had given us sixpence each—
And down we went to the beach.

We had sand in the eyes and the ears and the nose,
And sand in the hair, and sand-between-the-toes,
Whenever a good nor'-wester blows,
Christopher is certain of
Sand-between-the-toes.

The sea was galloping grey and white;
Christopher clutched his sixpence tight;
We clambered over the humping sand—
And Christopher held my hand.

We had sand in the eyes and the ears and the nose,
And sand in the hair, and sand-between-the-toes.
Whenever a good nor'-wester blows,
Christopher is certain of
Sand-between-the-toes.

There was a roaring in the sky;
The sea-gulls cried as they blew by.
We tried to talk, but had to shout—
Nobody else was out.

When we got home, we had sand in the hair,
In the eyes and the ears and everywhere;
Whenever a good nor'-wester blows,
Christopher is found with
Sand-between-the-toes.

A.A. Milne

A DRAGONFLY

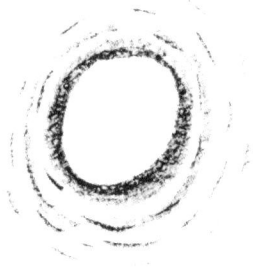

When the heat of summer
Made drowsy the land
A dragonfly came
And sat on my hand.
With its blue jointed body
And wings like spun glass
It lit on my fingers
As though they were grass.

Eleanor Farjeon

SWALLOW

Fly away, fly away over the sea,
Sun-loving swallow, for summer is done;
Come again, come again, come back to me,
Bringing the summer and bringing the sun.

Christina Rossetti

The Rainy Summer

There's much afoot in heaven and earth this year;
The winds hunt up the sun, hunt up the moon,
Trouble the dubious dawn, hasten the drear
Height of a threatening noon.

No breath of boughs, no breath of leaves, of fronds
May linger or grow warm; the trees are loud;
The forest, rooted, tosses her bonds,
And strains against the cloud.

No scents may pause within the garden-fold;
The rifled flowers are cold as ocean-shells;
Bees, humming in the storm, carry their cold
Wild honey to cold cells.

Alice Meynell

THE WHEAT RIPENING

What time the wheat field tinges rusty brown
And barley bleaches in its mellow grey
Tis sweet some smooth mown baulh* to wander down
Or cross the fields on footpaths narrow way
Just in the mealy light of waking day
As glittering dewdrops moist the maiden's gown
And sparkling bounces from her nimble feet
Journeying to milking from the neighbouring town
Making life bright with song—and it is sweet
To mark the grazing herds and list the clown
Urge on his ploughing team with cheering calls
And merry shepherds whistling toils begun
And hoarse tongued bird boy whose unceasing calls
Join the larks ditty to the rising sun.

John Clare

* A ridge between two furrows

THE PROVIDER

The tender grass grows up at God's command
    to feed the cattle,
And there are fruit trees, vegetables and grain
For man to cultivate, and wine to make him glad,
And olive oil as lotion for his skin,
And bread to give him strength.

From the Book of Psalms

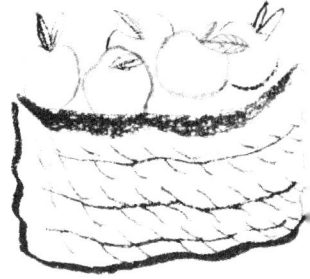

THE HARVEST

The silver rain, the shining sun,
The fields where scarlet poppies run,
And all the ripples of the wheat
Are in the bread that I do eat.

So when I sit for every meal
And say a grace, I always feel
That I am eating rain and sun,
And fields where scarlet poppies run.

Alice C. Henderson

GOODBYE TO SUMMER

Summer is gone with all its roses,
Its sun and perfume and sweet flowers,
Its warm air and refreshing showers:
And even Autumn closes.

Yea, Autumn's chilly self is going,
And winter comes which is much colder;
Each day the hoar-frost waxes bolder,
And the last buds cease blowing.

Christina Rossetti

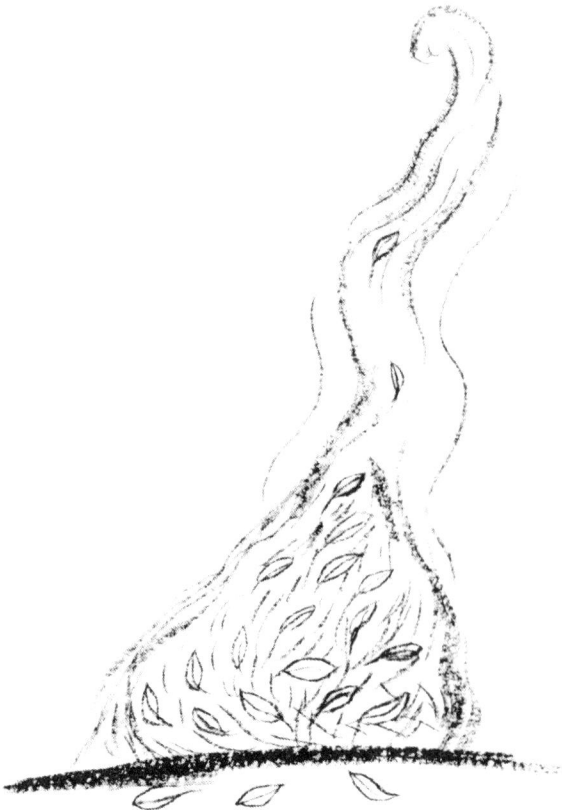

AUTUMN FIRES

In the other gardens
And all up the vale,
From the autumn bonfires
See the smoke trail!

Pleasant summer over
And all the summer flowers,
The red fire blazes,
The grey smoke towers.

Sing a song of seasons!
Something bright in all!
Flowers in the summer,
Fires in the fall!

Robert Louis Stevenson

THE FIELDMOUSE

Where the acorn tumbles down,
Where the ash tree sheds its berry,
With your fur so soft and brown,
With your eye so round and merry,
Scarcely moving the long grass,
Fieldmouse, I can see you pass.

Little thing, in what dark den,
Lie you all the winter sleeping?
Till warm weather comes again
Then once more I see you creeping
Round about the tall tree roots,
Nibbling at their fallen fruits.

Fieldmouse, fieldmouse, do not go,
Where the farmer stacks his treasure,
Find the nut that falls below,
Eat the acorn at your pleasure,
But you must not steal the grain
He has stacked with so much pain.

Make you a hole where mosses spring,
Underneath the tall oak's shadow,
Pretty, quiet, harmless thing,
Play about the sunny meadow.
Keep away from corn and house,
None will harm you, little mouse.

Cecil Frances Alexander

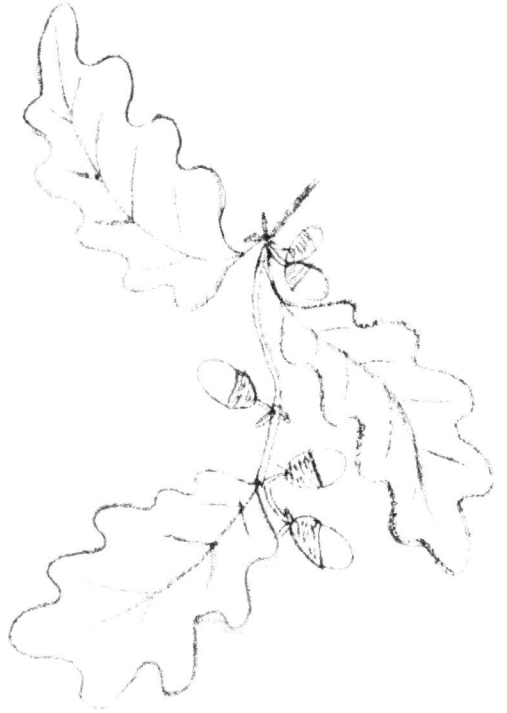

SOMETHING TOLD THE WILD GEESE

Something told the wild geese
It was time to go.
Though the fields lay golden,
Something whispered—'Snow.'
Leaves were green and stirring,
Berries, luster-glossed,
But beneath warm feathers,
Something cautioned—'Frost.'
All the sagging orchards
Steamed with amber spice,
But each wild breast stiffened
At remembered ice.
Something told the wild geese
It was time to fly—
Summer sun was on their wings,
Winter in their cry.

Rachel Field

A November Morning

The golden leaves, the little robin,
The yellow-hammer, the little brownie sparrow—
And the yellow sun sparkled like gold on the green leaves.

The funny old pigeon, who sat staring at us,
Blinked with his two little beady eyes.
He stayed staring at us
For quite a little time.
Then with a flash like a whole tree falling,
The pigeon flew away!

Then we went away somewhere
And when we came back we saw it again
Standing,
Staring at us,
And blinking with its two little beady eyes.
And then
In a little while
It slowly walked away.

So we went home.

Nicholas (aged 5)

SONG AT THE BEGINNING OF AUTUMN

Now watch this autumn that arrives
In smells. All looks like summer still;
Colours are quite unchanged, the air
On green and white serenely thrives.
Heavy the trees with growth and full
The fields. Flowers flourish everywhere.

But I am carried back against
My will into a childhood where
Autumn is bonfires, marbles, smoke;
I lean against my window fenced
From evocations in the air.
When I said autumn, autumn broke.

Elizabeth Jennings

THE AUTUMN ROBIN

Sweet little bird in russet coat,
The livery of the closing year,
I love thy lonely plaintive note
And tiny whispering song
    to hear,
While on the stile or garden seat
I sit to watch the falling leaves,
The song thy little joys repeat
My loneliness relieves.

John Clare

AUTUMN'S HARVEST

Red, golden leaves
And berries red,
Well garnered sheaves
And gossamer thread
O'er stubbles spread.
When all is said
'Tis the crown of the year
When Autumn's here.

Beach Thomas

AUTUMN

I love the fitful gust that shakes
The casement all the day,
And from the glossy elm tree takes
The faded leaves away,
Twirling them by the window pane
With thousand others down the lane.

I love to see the cottage smoke
Curl upward through the trees;
The pigeons nestled round the cote
On November days like these;
The cock upon the dunghill crowing
The mill sails on the heath a-going.

John Clare

A Squirrel

Slept through the winter, comes out at spring,
Quickly and quietly up the tree,
He peeps through a hole, oh what can he see,
Acorns and nuts on the old oak tree,
Spinning down the trunk and up the oak,
Oh happy he is today!
Oh happy he is today!

Feasting on nuts and acorns galore,
Drinking the fresh rain water pure,
Returns to his home a sweet little drey,
Of leaves, twigs and moss gathered that day,
Now he's ready for winter again,
It's winter time again.

Abigail Keeling (aged 8)

Address to a Child During a Boisterous Winter Evening

What way does the wind come? What way does he go?
He rides over the water, and over the snow,
Through wood and through vale; and o'er rocky height
Which the goat cannot climb, takes his sounding flight
He tosses about in every bare tree,
As, if you look up, you plainly may see;
But how he will come, and whither he goes,
There's never a scholar in England knows.

He will suddenly stop in a cunning nook,
And ring a sharp 'larum—but if you should look,
There's nothing to see but a cushion of snow
Round as a pillow, and whiter than milk,
And softer than if it were covered in silk.
Sometimes he'll hide in the cave of a rock,
Then whistle as shrill as the buzzard cock;
Yet seek him—and what shall you find in the place?
Nothing but silence and empty space;
Save, in a corner, a heap of dry leaves,
That he's left for a bed, to beggars or thieves.

Dorothy Wordsworth

The Coming

Here it comes!
After a year of waiting.
It swirls down on earth like a whirlwind,
Slow at first, trickling through the clouds,
Then faster and faster,
Glistening and sparkling,
Throwing itself against the windows.
And then ceases
Forming a white crunchy carpet for us to walk on.

Sophie (aged 10)

WHITE FIELDS

In winter-time we go
Walking in the fields of snow;

Where there is no grass at all;
Where the top of every wall,

Every fence and every tree,
Is as white as white can be.

Pointing out the way we came—
Every one of them the same—

All across the fields there be
Prints in silver filigree;

And our mothers always know,
By the footprints in the snow,
Where it is the children go.

James Stephens

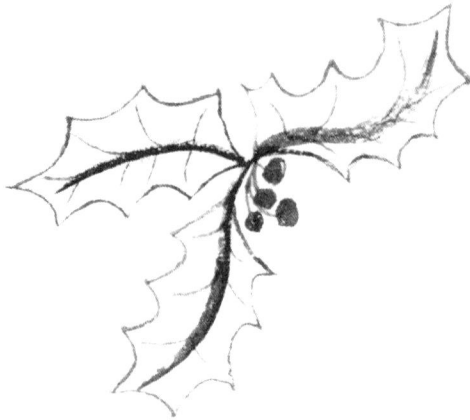

Special Days

CHRISTMAS DAYBREAK

Before the paling of the stars,
Before the winter morn,
Before the earliest cockcrow,
Jesus Christ was born:
Born in a stable,
Cradled in a manger,
In the world His hands had made,
Born a stranger.

Priest and king lay fast asleep
In Jerusalem,
Young and old lay fast asleep
In crowded Bethlehem.
Saint and angel, ox and ass,
Kept a watch together,
Before the Christmas daybreak
In the winter weather.

Jesus on His Mother's breast
In the stable cold,
Spotless Lamb of God was He,
Shepherd of the fold.
Let us kneel with Mary Maid,
With Joseph bent and hoary,
With saint and angel, ox and ass,
To Hail the King of Glory.

Christina Rossetti

THE FIRST MERCY

Ox and ass at Bethlehem
On a night ye know of them;
We were only creatures small
Hid by shadows on the wall.

We were swallow, moth and mouse;
The Child was born in our house,
And the bright eyes of us three
Peeped at His Nativity.

Hands of peace upon that place
Hushed our beings for a space—
Quiet feet and folded wing,
Nor a sound of anything.

With a moving star we crept
Closer when the Baby slept:
Men who guarded where He lay
Moved to frighten us away.

But the Babe, awakened, laid,
Love on things that were afraid,
With so sweet a gesture He
Called us to His company.

Bruce Blunt

CHRISTMAS BELLS

I heard the bells on Christmas Day
Their old familiar carols play,
And wild and sweet
The words repeat,
Of 'Peace on earth, good will to men!'

And thought how, as the day had come,
The belfries of all Christendom
Had rolled along
The unbroken song,
Of 'Peace on earth, good will to men!'

Till ringing, singing on its way,
The world revolved from night to day—
A voice, a chime,
A chant sublime,
Of 'Peace on earth, good will to men!'

And in despair I bowed my head;
'There is no peace on earth,' I said,
For hate is strong
And mocks the song
Of peace on earth, good will to men!

Then pealed the bells more loud and deep:
'God is not dead; nor doth He sleep!
The wrong shall fail,
The right prevail,
With peace on earth, good will to men!'

H.W. Longfellow

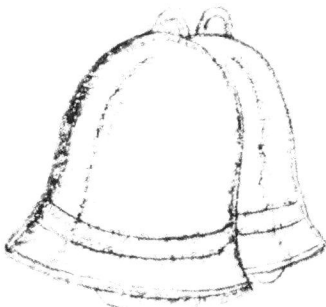

CHESTER CAROL

He who made the earth so fair
Slumbers in a stable bare,
Warmed by cattle standing there.

Oxen, lowing, stand all round;
In the stall no other sound
Mars the peace by Mary found.

Joseph piles the soft, sweet hay,
Starlight drives the dark away,
Angels sing a heavenly lay.

Jesus sleeps in Mary's arm;
Sheltered there from harsh alarm,
None can do him ill or harm.

See His mother o'er Him bend;
Hers the joy to soothe and tend,
Hers the bliss that knows no end.

Anon

THE SHEPHERD'S CAROL

We stood on the hills, Lady,
Our day's work done,
Watching the frosted meadows
That winter had won.

The evening was calm, Lady,
The air so still,
Silence more lovely than music
Folded the hill.

There was a star, Lady,
Shone in the night,
Larger than Venus it was
And bright, so bright.

Oh, a voice from the sky, Lady,
It seemed to us then
Telling of God being born
In the world of men.

And so we have come, Lady,
Our day's work done,
Our love, our hopes, ourselves
We give to your son.

Anon

THE GIFT

It was an insignificant
little package
and there was some doubt
about its origin.

Somehow
the local yokels
knew about its arrival
and even
more surprisingly
so did some
foreign boffins.

The contents
seemed ordinary enough
but its survival
in the face of a royal decree
to destroy
any similar deliveries
was remarkable.

Perhaps it was because
this particular package
came under special security
direct from the manufacturer.
It was His instructions
and a guarantee for life.

Sarah Aston

THE JOY OF GIVING

Somehow, not only for Christmas
But all the long year through,
The joy you give to others
Is the joy that comes back to you:
And the more you spend in blessing
The poor and lonely and sad,
The more of your heart's possessing
Returns to make you glad.

John Greenleaf Whittier

TO WELCOME IN THE YEAR

Little Boy
Full of joy;
Little Girl,
Sweet and small;
Cock does crow,
So do you;
Merry voice,
Infant noise,
Merrily, Merrily, to welcome in the Year.

William Blake

THE OLD YEAR

Farewell old year,
With goodness crowned,
A hand divine hath set thy bound.

Welcome New Year,
Which shall bring
Fresh blessing from
Our Lord and King.

The old we leave without a tear,
The new we enter without fear.

Anon

THE PANCAKE

Mix a pancake,
Stir a pancake,
Pop it in the pan.

Fry the pancake,
Toss the pancake,
Catch it if you can.

Christina Rossetti

White Lent

Now quit your care
And anxious fear and worry:
For schemes are vain
And fretting brings no gain.
To prayer, to prayer!
Bells call and clash and hurry,
In Lent the bells do cry,
'Come buy, come buy,
Come buy with love the love most high!'

Lent comes in the spring,
And spring is pied with brightness;
The sweetest flowers,
Keen winds, and sun and showers,
Their health do bring
To make Lent's chastened whiteness;
For life to men brings light
And might, and might,
And might to those whose hearts are right.

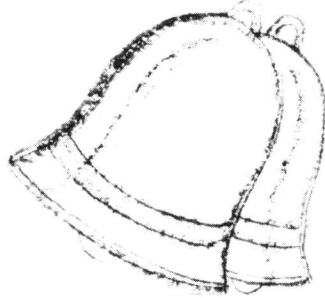

For righteousness
And peace will show their faces
To those who feed
The hungry in their need,
And wrongs redress,
Who build the old waste places,
And in the darkness shine,
Divine, divine,
Divine it is when all combine.

Then shall your light
Break forth as doth the morning;
Your health shall spring,
The friends you make shall bring
God's glory bright,
Your way through life adorning;
And love shall be the prize.
Arise, arise,
Arise and make a paradise.

Percy Dearmer

MOTHERING SUNDAY

It is the day of all the year,
Of all the year the one day,
When I shall see my mother dear
And bring her cheer,
A-mothering on Sunday.

So I'll put on my Sunday coat,
And in my hat a feather,
And get the lines I writ by rote
With many a note,
That I've a-strung together.

And now to fetch my wheaten cake,*
To fetch it from the baker,
He promised me, for mother's sake,
The best he'd bake
For me to fetch and take her.

* the custom is now to bake a simnel cake

Well have I known, as I went by
One hollow lane, that none day
I'd fail to find—for all they're shy—
Where violets lie,
As I went home on Sunday.

My sister Jane is waiting-maid
Along with Squire's lady;
And year by year her part she's played,
And home she stayed,
To get the dinner ready.

For mother'll come to church, you'll see—
Of all the year it's the day—
'The one,' she'll say, 'that's made for me.'
And so it be:
It's every mother's free day.

The boys will all come home from town,
Not one will miss that one day:
And every maid will bustle down
To show her gown,
A-mothering on Sunday.

It is the day of all the year,
Of all the year the one day;
And here come I, my mother dear,
To bring you cheer,
A-mothering on Sunday.

George Hare Leonard

EASTER SONG

Spring bursts today,
For Christ is risen and all the earth's at play.

Flash forth, thou sun,
The rain is over and gone, its work done.

Winter is past,
Sweet spring is come at last, is come at last.

Bud, fig and vine,
Bud, olive, fat with fruit and oil and wine.

Break forth this morn
In roses, thou but yesterday a thorn.

Uplift thy head,
O pure white lily through the winter dead.

Beside your dams
Leap and rejoice, you merry-making lambs.

All herds and flocks
Rejoice, all beasts of thickets and of rocks.

Sing, creatures, sing,
Angels and men and birds, and everything.

Christina Rossetti

EASTER

In the sky
The song of the skylark
Greets the dawn.
In the fields wet with dew
The scent of the violets
Fills the air.
On such a lovely morning as this
Surely on such a lovely morning as this
Lord Jesus
Came forth
From the tomb.

Misuno Genzo

EASTER

Birds nesting
Grass growing
Leaves budding
Wind blowing

Soldiers marching
Jesus dying
Peter sobbing
Mary crying

Sunday dawning
Jesus living
Friends running
No more grieving.

Wendy Green

Easter Wings

Lord who createst man in wealth and store,
though foolishly he lost the same,
decaying more and more,
till he became
most poor,
with thee.
Oh let me rise,
as larks, harmoniously,
and sing this day thy victories:
then shall that fall further the flight in me.
My tender age in sorrow did begin,
and still with sicknesses and shame
thou didst so punish sin
that I became
most thin.
With thee
let me combine,
and feel this day thy victory:
for, if I graft my wing on thine,
affliction shall advance the flight in me.

George Herbert

WHEN MARY THRO' THE GARDEN WENT*

When Mary thro' the garden went
There was no sound of any bird,
And yet, because the night was spent,
The little grasses lightly stirred,
The flowers awoke, the lilies heard.

When Mary thro' the garden went,
The dew lay still on flower and grass,
The waving palms about her sent
Their fragrance out as she did pass,
No light upon the branches was.

When Mary thro' the garden went,
Her eyes, for weeping long, were dim,
The grass beneath her footsteps bent,
The solemn lilies, white and slim,
These also stood and wept for him.

When Mary thro' the garden went,
She sought, within the garden ground,
One for whom her heart was rent,
One who for her sake was bound,
One who sought and she was found.

Mary E. Coleridge

* *This poem uses an abbreviated form of 'through'*

THERE WAS NO

There was no grave grave enough
to ground me
to mound me
I broke the balm then slit the shroud
wound round me
that bound me

There was no death dead enough
to dull me
to cull me
I snapped the snake and waned his war
to lull me
to null me

there was no cross cross enough
to nil me
to still me
I hung as gold that bled, and bloomed
A rose that rose and prised the tomb
away from Satan's wilful doom
There was no cross, death, grave
or room
to hold me.

Stewart Henderson

GOLDEN SHEAVES

Sing to the Lord of harvest,
Sing songs of love and praise;
With joyful hearts and voices
Your alleluyas raise:
By him the rolling seasons
In fruitful order move,
Sing to the Lord of harvest
A song of happy love.

Sing to the Lord of harvest,
The deserts bloom and spring,
The hills leap up in gladness,
The valleys laugh and sing;
He filleth with his fulness
All things with large increase,
He crowns the year with goodness
With plenty and with peace.

J.S.B. Monsell

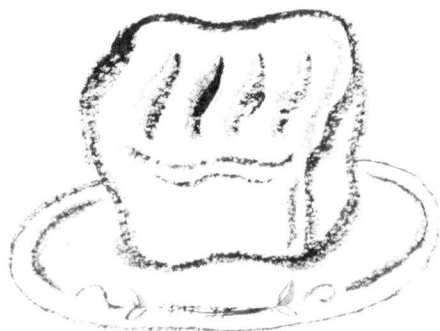

HARVEST

I saw the farmer plough the field,
And row on row
The furrows grow.
I saw the farmer plough the field,
And hungry furrows grow.

I saw the farmer sow the wheat,
The golden grain,
In sun and rain,
I saw the farmer sow the wheat,
In shining sun and rain.

I saw at first a silvery sheen,
Then line on line
Of living green.
I saw at first a silvery sheen,
Then lines of living green.

The living green then turned to gold,
In thirty—fifty—
Hundred fold.
The living green then turned to gold
In mercies manifold.

M.M. Hutchinson

A Harvest Blessing

Bread is a lovely thing to eat—
God bless the barley and the wheat!

A lovely thing to breathe is air—
God bless the sunshine everywhere!

The earth's a lovely place to know—
God bless the folks that come and go!

Alive's a lovely thing to be—
Giver of life—we say—God bless Thee!

H.M. Sarson

In Due Season

There is a right time for everything:
A time to be born; a time to die;
A time to plant; a time to harvest;
A time to kill; a time to heal;
A time to destroy; a time to rebuild;
A time to cry; a time to laugh;
A time to grieve; a time to dance;
A time for scattering stones; a time for gathering stones;
A time to hug; a time not to hug;
A time to find; a time to lose;
A time for keeping; a time for throwing away;
A time to tear; a time to repair;
A time to be quiet; a time to speak up;
A time for loving; a time for hating;
A time for war; a time for peace.

From the Book of Ecclesiastes

SUBJECT INDEX

INDEX OF FIRST LINES

ACKNOWLEDGMENTS

We would like to thank all those who have given us permission to include quotations in this book, as indicated in the list below, and the children whose poems are acknowledged elsewhere. Every effort has been made to trace and acknowledge copyright holders of all the quotations included in this book. We apologize for any errors or omissions that may remain, and would ask those concerned to contact the publishers, who will ensure that full acknowledgment is made in the future.

'The Gift' © Sarah Aston, used by permission of the author. 'White Lent' by Percy Dearmer, from *The Oxford Book of Carols*. © Oxford University Press 1928. 'A Dragonfly' © Eleanor Farjeon, from *Silver Sand and Snow*, published by Michael Joseph. Used by permission of David Higham Associates Ltd. 'Easter' © Wendy Green, used by permission of the author. 'There Was No' © Stewart Henderson, used by permission of the author. 'Song at the Beginning of Autumn' © Elizabeth Jennings, from *The Poems*, published by Carcanet. Used by permission of David Higham Associates Ltd. Extracts from *The Living Bible* © 1971 used by permission of Kingsway Publications, Eastbourne, East Sussex BN23 6NT. 'April Rise' © Laurie Lee, from *Collected Poems*, published by Penguin Books. Reprinted by permission of the Peters Fraser & Dunlop Group Ltd. 'Mothering Sunday' by George Hare Leonard, from *The Oxford Book of Carols*. © Oxford University Press 1928. 'Sand-Between-the-Toes' © A.A. Milne, from *When We Were Very Young*, published by Methuen Children's Books. Reprinted by permission of Reed Consumer Books Ltd. 'White Fields' © James Stephens, reprinted by permission of The Society of Authors as the Literary Representatives of the Estate of James Stephens. 'Seasons' © Steve Turner, from *The Day I Fell Down the Toilet*, Lion Publishing plc. 'Spring Has Come', translation by Steuart Wilson, from *The Oxford Book of Carols*. © Oxford University Press 1928.